Cooking Up Fun in the Kitchen

Emilie Barnes

WITH ANNE CHRISTIAN BUCHANAN

Illustrations by Michal Sparks

HARVEST HOUSE PUBLISHERS
Eugene, Oregon

Cooking Up Fun in the Kitchen

Text Copyright © 2000 Emilie Barnes and Anne Christian Buchanan
Published by Harvest House Publishers
Eugene, Oregon 97402

Mr. Gifford Bowne
Indigo Gate
1 Pegasus Drive
Colts Neck, NJ 07722
(732) 577-9333

Design and Production by Garborg Design Works, Minneapolis, Minnesota

Library of Congress Cataloging-in-Publication Data

Barnes, Emilie.
    Cooking up fun in the kitchen / Emilie Barnes with Anne Christian Buchanan; illustrations by Michal Sparks.
        p. cm.
    Summary: Presents recipes for breakfast, lunch, and dinner, from homemade spaghetti sauce to tangy tuna
    ISBN 0-7369-0131-0
    1. Cookery—Juvenile literature. [1. Cookery.] I. Title. II. Buchanan, Anne Christian. III. Sparks, Michal, ill.

TX652 .B3196 2000
641.5'123 21—dc21   99-044130

Printed in the United States of America

00 01 02 03 04 05 06 07 08 09 10 / IP / 10 9 8 7 6 5 4 3 2 1

Contents

Cookin' Up Some Double Fun!

4

Hi, I'm Emilie Marie, and I wish you could see my friends and me right now!

Christine has little splats of cake batter all over her—and even a big splat on her nose.

So does Maria. She even has a little flour in her hair!

Aleesha and Elizabeth have red spatters on their aprons, plus a little on their faces.

I have chocolate smears on my apron and in the corners of my mouth.

In fact, the only one who looks pretty clean is Jasmine, although she's got little bits of lettuce all over her hands. (She's making the salad!)

What are we doing? Well, as you may know, we're all in a club together, the Angels. And right now we're in the middle of one of our favorite club projects: We're making dinner for our families. Spaghetti and meat sauce. And twisty, buttery breadsticks. And a big salad with ranch dressing. And even yellow cupcakes baked in ice-cream cones, with yummy chocolate frosting.

We can't wait to eat it all—after we clean up, of course. But do you know what? Making it is almost as much fun as eating it!

Do you like to cook? I do—a lot. My friends like to cook, too. In fact, one of our favorite things to do on a rainy Saturday or a school-day afternoon is get together in the kitchen and cook up something really yummy. Last summer, in fact, we decided to make cooking our summer project. Once a week we got together at one of our houses and learned to make something new.

Boy, did we learn a lot over the summer. We learned to make dishes for breakfast, lunch, and dinner. We learned to make yummy snacks. We even invented a few recipes of our own. This book tells you some of the things we've learned to do—so you can do them, too.

But we didn't do it all by ourselves, of course. We had lots of help. My mom and my Grammie are really good cooks and good teachers, too, so we learned a lot from them. So is Maria's dad—he's a baker, and he really knows a lot about making good breads and cakes and stuff like that.

Jasmine's mom is a whiz at garnishes—that's decorating food to make it look pretty. Christine's mom showed us how to make pretty pancakes. And Aleesha's dad is the king of spaghetti—plus he makes a really great salad. (Now *we* know how to make great salad, too!)

And do you know what we like best about cooking? It's double fun!

First you have the fun of making it.

Then you have the fun of eating it.

And the most fun of all is making and eating it with your friends!

We hope our very own cookbook brings all that fun into your life!

CHAPTER 1

The Kitchen Rules!

HOW TO COOK ALMOST ANYTHING—THE BASICS

We Angels have learned we can make almost anything if we have a recipe, some common sense, and sometimes a little help! Here are some basic steps to follow when you're having fun in the kitchen.

1. **Read the recipe—the whole thing.** This is really important! That way, you'll know what's coming up and you'll be ready. It even helps to read it two times before you ever start. If there's something you don't understand, check the "how-tos" at the back of this book or ask an adult to show you how. Be sure and think about how long the recipe will take and how many people it will serve. You might need to choose another, faster recipe. Or maybe you need to double a recipe— make twice as much of it. (That's in the how-tos, too.)

2. **Have an adult standing by.** That means your mom or dad or grandmother—whoever is in charge of your kitchen. Ask for permission to use the kitchen, and ask the adult to stand by to help you with things like boiling water and sharp knives. An adult assistant can also help you figure out how to change a recipe if you don't understand something or don't have everything you need.

3. **Wash your hands and put on an apron.** This is just good common sense—to protect your clothes and keep the food clean. Be sure to wash well, with soap. Also be sure to wash your hands after you've handled any kind of meat. Wash the utensils and cutting surfaces, too.

4. **Gather all your ingredients together before you start.** (Ingredients are the foods that go together in the recipe.) We've listed them at the beginning of each recipe, so that's easy. First, check your

cabinets to see what's there—or ask your adult assistant if there's something else you can use. You might need to make a list and go shopping!

5. **Gather all your cooking tools—like mixing bowls and spoons and pots and pans—ahead of time.** I've listed them at the beginning of each recipe, too. If you don't have a certain piece of equipment in your house, ask your adult for something else you can use. Maybe you can even go next door and borrow something!

6. **Preheat the oven if you need to.** Of course, you'll only do this if the recipe uses the oven—but you'll know that because you've read the recipe, right? An oven thermometer can help you know if your oven is too hot or too cold—and that can really make a difference.

7. **When everything's ready, follow** the recipe step by step. It's easy if you do one thing at a time!

8. **Clean up as you go.** When you're waiting for something to cook or rise, take that time to put away the ingredients and utensils you've finished with so cleanup won't take so long. My Grammie taught me to run some soapy water in the sink. That way I can put the dirty dishes in right away and get them cleaned up.

9. **Think pretty!** Some food you'll want to gobble up right away. Some food you'll serve to your family as a meal. Some food you'll cover and save for later, and some you'll even give as a gift. Whatever you do, take a minute and think about how you'll serve it. Maybe you can

Symbols to Watch for in This Book

Watch for the following symbols all through this book. They're telling you something you need to know or do!

means you need to ask an adult to help you because this step could be dangerous.

means that if you don't know how to do something, the "How-tos and Helpful Hints" in the back of the book will show you how.

means this recipe uses something made by another recipe.

make it prettier by arranging it nicely on the plate or adding a garnish—that's a food decoration! We've added some ideas in this book for making everything pretty.

10. Clean up completely when you're finished! Your fun in the kitchen isn't really done until the ingredients and equipment are back in the cabinets, everything that's dirty has been washed (including your face and hands!), and the stove and countertops are clean.

11. Enjoy. When you're through with cooking fun—it's time to get started with the eating fun!

8

How to Stay

Kitchens are fun, but they can also be dangerous. Here are some things to be careful about.

- Always work with clean hands, a clean work surface, and clean utensils.

- If you have long hair, tie it back—or put it up under a great chef's hat!

- Wipe up spills right away—so no one trips and falls.

- Hot steam can burn you. When you open a pan lid, open it away from you so that the steam goes away from your face. If you've cooked something in the microwave with plastic wrap on the top, carefully use a pot holder to pull up a corner of the wrap away from you. Keep arms and face away whenever you put cold liquid into a hot pan—and ask an adult to help you whenever you must pour boiling water.

Safe While You're Doing It

- Bacteria can grow in food that's left out too long, and bacteria can make you sick. That's why you should always thaw frozen foods in the refrigerator or microwave, not out on the counter. Also, when you've finished cooking something, don't leave it sitting out on the counter for more than an hour. Cover it and put it in the refrigerator.

- Raw meat can carry bacteria, too, although cooking kills the bacteria. If you handle raw meat, be sure and scrub your hands, the counter, utensils, and cutting boards before using with other food. If possible, use different cutting boards for meat and veggies. And always cook meat until all the pink has disappeared from the middle.

- Always use thick, dry pot holders to touch hot pans and lids. Never pick up a pan with a damp or wet pot holder or one that is worn thin—you could get burned.

- Don't let paper towels or pot holders get near the stove burners. Don't let electrical cords dangle or get wet. This way, you'll avoid fire or electrical shock.

- Ask your mom or dad what you should do if a cooking fire starts. It doesn't happen very often, but it's good to know!

- Always ask for help if you need it. You need it for using sharp knives, electrical appliances, stoves or ovens.

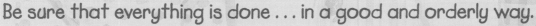

Be sure that everything is done . . . in a good and orderly way.

THE BOOK OF 1 CORINTHIANS

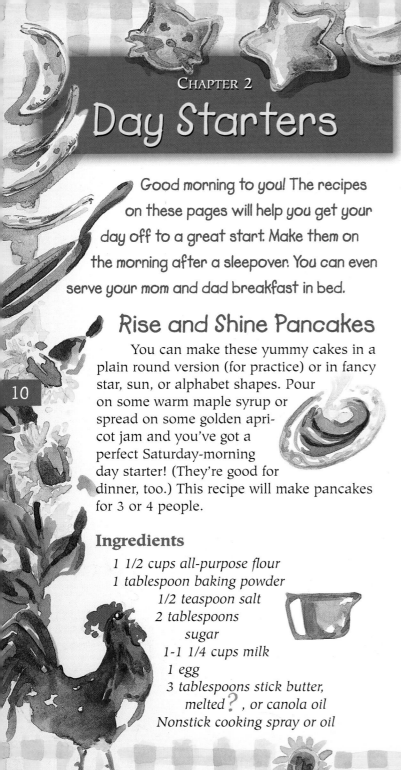

CHAPTER 2

Day Starters

Good morning to you! The recipes on these pages will help you get your day off to a great start. Make them on the morning after a sleepover. You can even serve your mom and dad breakfast in bed.

Rise and Shine Pancakes

You can make these yummy cakes in a plain round version (for practice) or in fancy star, sun, or alphabet shapes. Pour on some warm maple syrup or spread on some golden apricot jam and you've got a perfect Saturday-morning day starter! (They're good for dinner, too.) This recipe will make pancakes for 3 or 4 people.

Ingredients

1 1/2 cups all-purpose flour
1 tablespoon baking powder
1/2 teaspoon salt
2 tablespoons sugar
1-1 1/4 cups milk
1 egg
3 tablespoons stick butter, melted ? , or canola oil
Nonstick cooking spray or oil

Cooking Tools

Griddle or large flat frying pan (skillet)
Large and small mixing bowls
Large and small spoons
Wire whisk
Measuring cups and spoons
Basting brush (if using oil instead of nonstick spray)
Cup or ladle (for round pancakes)
Clean plastic squeeze bottle (the kind mustard or ketchup comes in, for fancy pancakes)
Funnel or small spoon
Ovenproof plate or flat dish
Sheet of aluminum foil or large metal bowl

How to Make It

1. Put the griddle or skillet on a stove burner and turn the heat to medium-high. Let it heat up while you mix the pancake batter.

2. Measure the flour, baking powder, salt, and sugar ? together in a large bowl. Use a spoon or a whisk to stir these dry ingredients all together.

3. In a smaller bowl, combine the milk, egg, and melted butter (or oil). Beat with a wire whisk until thoroughly combined.

4. With your fingers, make a little well in the flour mixture in the large bowl. Pour the milk, egg, and butter mixture into the well, then stir with

the whisk until all the flour is wet. Don't keep on stirring after that. The batter can be a little lumpy.

5. Now check to see if the griddle is the right temperature. Dip your fingers in some water and splash a few drops onto the griddle. The drops should dance around and sizzle and disappear after a few seconds. If they just lie there, the griddle isn't hot enough. If they evaporate right away, the griddle is too hot. Turn the heat up or down if you need to and test the griddle again in a few minutes. When the griddle is just right, spray it with a little cooking spray or brush on a little oil.

6. To make a plain round pancake, pour about 1/4 cup of batter onto the griddle. (You can actually pour it from the measuring cup.) With a spoon or the bottom of the cup, spread the batter around just a little to make a circle about 4 to 5 inches across. The pancake will start cooking right away. In a few minutes, you'll see that the edges look a little dry instead of all shiny, and bubbles will start to pop on the surface of the pancake. When that happens, lift the edge with a spatula and look under it. If it's brown, carefully slip the spatula under the pancake, lift it up, and turn it over. Press down a little on the top and let the pancake cook just about a minute more—until that side is brown, too. (It probably won't get as brown as the first side.) Then pick the pancake up with the

spatula and put it on an ovenproof plate. Don't turn the pancake over and over in the pan. Cook it once on each side.

7. Turn on the oven very low—about 200 degrees. Put the plate with the pancake in the oven to stay warm while you make more pancakes. Cover loosely with a sheet of aluminum foil or a metal bowl. Put each pancake on the plate in the oven after you make it.

8. After you make a couple of plain round pancakes for practice, you're ready to start making fun pancake shapes. Here's how to do them. First, take the lid off the squeeze bottle and use a funnel or a small spoon to put the batter into the bottle. Put the lid back on. Tap the bottom of the bottle on the counter a few times to get out any air bubbles. Then hold the bottle upside down over a bowl and shake a few times to move the batter down into the nozzle. Now you're ready to make creative pancake shapes. All you have to do is squeeze a line of batter onto the hot griddle into a shape. Squeeze an outline first and then, if you want to, fill it in with a little batter. It takes a little practice at first! Then finish cooking as you did for round pancakes. Turn them carefully, because little pieces can break off.

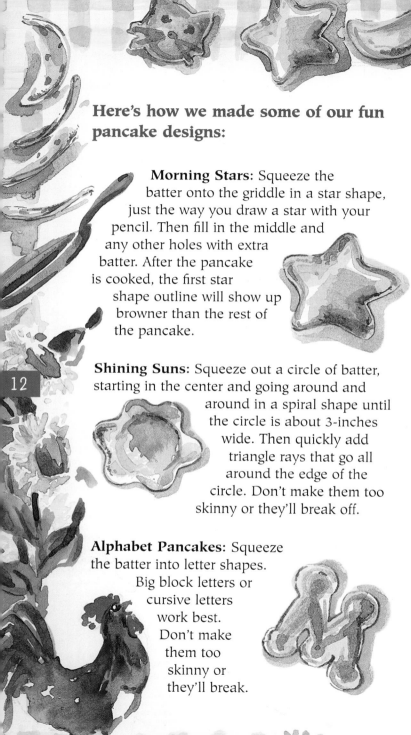

Here's how we made some of our fun pancake designs:

Morning Stars: Squeeze the batter onto the griddle in a star shape, just the way you draw a star with your pencil. Then fill in the middle and any other holes with extra batter. After the pancake is cooked, the first star shape outline will show up browner than the rest of the pancake.

Shining Suns: Squeeze out a circle of batter, starting in the center and going around and around in a spiral shape until the circle is about 3-inches wide. Then quickly add triangle rays that go all around the edge of the circle. Don't make them too skinny or they'll break off.

Alphabet Pancakes: Squeeze the batter into letter shapes. Big block letters or cursive letters work best. Don't make them too skinny or they'll break.

12

Good-for-You Turkey Sausage

This yummy sausage goes great with your pancakes. This recipe will make sausage for 4-6 people.

Ingredients

1 pound ground turkey
1/2 teaspoon nutmeg
1/2 teaspoon sage
1/2 teaspoon thyme
1/8 teaspoon cayenne pepper (or less)
1 teaspoon salt

Cooking Tools

Skillet or 9 x 13 baking pan
Spatula
Kitchen timer

How to Make It

1. Mix all the ingredients together—it's easier to do it with your hands. Shape the meat into 12 small patties.

2. Put the patties in an ungreased skillet and cook them over medium heat until they are brown on one side. Turn them over with the spatula to brown other side. Or put them on a baking pan and bake at 350 degrees for 20-30 minutes, just until they are no longer pink on the inside. (Cut one open with a kitchen knife to check.)

Fun Ideas for Serving Breakfast

- Be creative about what you put on your pancakes. Instead of the traditional butter or syrup, try applesauce or peanut butter.

- Put your breakfast treats on a tray and treat someone special to breakfast in bed. Put a pretty cloth or placemat on the bottom of a large tray. Add china, glasses, flatware, and a colorful napkin tied with a ribbon. A little vase filled with flowers adds a special touch, too—try using an old pill bottle and a single daisy or rosebud.

- Wrap up your goodies in plastic containers, add juice boxes or thermoses, tuck in some picnic dishes and pretty napkins, and then you can take your happy wake-up anywhere you want.

- Here's a great "to go" dish for breakfast: Just make a big round pancake and wrap it around a couple of sausage patties or some scrambled eggs. Wrap it in foil to keep it warm. Then eat it like a burrito.

- For a delicious rosy breakfast drink, try mixing cranberry juice drink with orange juice.

- Who says you have to have breakfast for breakfast? As long as it's healthy, almost anything you like will help give you the energy you need for the day. Try a peanut butter and jelly sandwich on toast, some dinner leftovers heated in the microwave, some fruit and cheese, or even yesterday's pizza (warmed up). And while you're at it, offer to make pancakes and sausage for dinner!

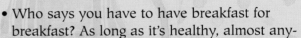
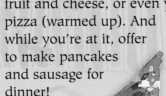

13

CHAPTER 3

Food to Go

Don't always get stuck with plain old bologna sandwiches for picnics and school lunches! Here are some other great ideas.

Tuna Two Ways

Just a few changes of ingredients can give a new twist to plain old tuna. Try these variations, then make up some of your own! One of these recipes will make about 2 cups of tuna—or lunch for 4 people.

Ingredients for the Basic Recipe

1 5-ounce can water-packed tuna (you can also make this recipe with cans of chicken)
1/4 cup celery, chopped ?
1/4 cup carrot, chopped ?
3 tablespoons mayonnaise or light mayonnaise
3 tablespoons nonfat plain yogurt
1 tablespoon lemon juice ?
1/4 teaspoon celery salt

Ingredients for Sweet 'n' Chunky Tuna

Basic recipe, plus:
1/4 of an apple, chopped ?
1/4 cup walnuts, chopped ?
1 green onion, sliced ?
1/2 cup seedless grapes, halved ?—you don't have to have these, but they're good!

Ingredients for Tangy Tuna

Basic recipe, plus:
2 tablespoons chopped pickle or pickle relish, whichever kind you like ?
1 hard-boiled egg, chopped
1 tablespoon Dijon mustard

Cooking Tools for Either Recipe

Can opener
Medium-sized bowl
Fork for flaking and mixing tuna
Cutting board and knife for chopping ingredients
Measuring spoons

How to Make It

1. To make the basic recipe, first open the can of tuna and drain off the liquid . Put the tuna in the bowl and break the big chunks apart with a fork. Then add all the other ingredients and stir well.

2. To make the Sweet 'n' Chunky Tuna or Tangy Tuna, just stir in the extra ingredients and mix really well. Store in covered containers in the refrigerator until ready to pack for your lunch or picnic. Spread it on wheat bread, tuck it in a pita, or just mound it on a lettuce leaf for a yummy salad.

How to Hard-Boil an Egg

Hard-boiled eggs are great travelers—just be sure to pack a little salt and pepper. You can make just one egg by this recipe, but you might as well make more and have some extras for tuna salad. This is also the way to prepare Easter Eggs for dying.

Ingredients

5-6 large eggs
Water

Cooking Tools

Medium-sized saucepan with a tight-fitting lid
Kitchen timer

How to Make It

1. Put the eggs in the bottom of a saucepan that has a tight lid. Add cold water deep enough to cover the eggs completely, plus a little more.

2. Place pan on the stove and turn on heat to medium high. Let heat for about five or ten minutes, then turn up heat to high.

3. When water boils, put the lid on the saucepan and remove the whole thing from the stove.  Put the pan on a heatproof surface and let it stand covered for 10 minutes. Then ask an adult to take the pan to the sink and drain off the hot water. Run cold water in the pan for several minutes to stop the eggs from cooking. Store them in the refrigerator.

Mix-and-Match Trail Mix

Trail mix is a good source of energy for hikes and other strenuous activities. You can buy it, but it's fun to mix your own from ingredients you like best. The recipe makes as much as you want to make!

Cooking Tools

A bowl for every ingredient, plus one large mixing bowl
Plastic bags

How to Make It

1. Put every ingredient you've collected into a different bowl. Then add handfuls from the small bowls into the big one, creating the kind of mixture you want.

2. Pack your trail mix in plastic bags for the road.

Possible Ingredients for Trail Mix

Roasted, unsalted nuts (peanuts, walnuts, pecans, almonds, mixed nuts)
Dried fruits (apples, apricots, raisins, dates, pineapple, cranberries)
Toasted seeds (sesame seeds, sunflower seeds, pumpkin seeds)
Extras (candy-coated chocolate candies, cereal)

Fun Ideas for Lunches and Picnics

- To keep your sandwiches from becoming soggy, spread both pieces of bread with a little butter or margarine before you put on the filling. Or pack the filling in a small plastic container and spread it on your bread after you arrive at your destination.

- If you're going on a picnic, take time to pack a pretty basket. If you're careful (and ask permission) you can even take real dishes and cloth napkins—or find some cute paper ones. Be sure to pack a tablecloth or blanket. And remember to use a thermal bag or ice pack to keep cold foods cold—and safe.

- One fun picnic idea is to have everyone pack a lunch to trade with someone else. Draw names from a hat and switch lunches. Be sure and pack the most delicious lunch you can think of.

- Sandwiches make great to-go foods, but they're not the only picnic possibilities. Try a leafy green salad with little chunks of chicken (tuck in an individual package of dressing from the produce aisle at the grocery store); cheese chunks, wheat crackers, and fresh fruit; leftover pieces of fried chicken; a thermos bottle full of soup or chili.

- If you and your friends like the same things on your sandwiches, try packing one loooong sandwich for a whole group. Just cut a loaf of French bread in half the long way and add sandwich fillings. Pack a serrated knife (with a zigzag edge) for cutting the sandwich into pieces.

- Dipper lunches are easy and fun. Use little plastic containers to pack dips such as cheese sauce, spaghetti sauce, whipped topping, or even chocolate. Dip in cut-up veggies, pieces of bread, cookies, or fruit.

- For a fun picnic experience, line the cups of an old egg carton with foil and put a different finger food in each cup. Try: banana slices tossed in orange juice (so they won't turn brown), grapes, mini-pretzels, cheese cubes, tiny cookies or crackers, raisins, boiled eggs, nuts, whatever you can think of. Then just close the carton and pack. Be sure and keep it right side up, though, so the ingredients won't spill out.

A happy heart makes the face cheerful.
THE BOOK OF PROVERBS

17

CHAPTER 4

Eating Your Veggies (and Liking It)

They're pretty and colorful and full of vitamins—and they can be yummy if you fix 'em right. Here are some veggies we like a lot.

Green and Leafy Salad Bowl

The best thing about salads (besides being pretty and good for you) is that you can make them any way you want. If you don't like an ingredient, just take it out. If you like one lettuce better than another, just switch. You can use any kind of dressing—clear, creamy, or none at all. And you really feel like a gourmet chef when you're tossing that beautiful, colorful bowl of goodness! This recipe makes salad for about 4 people.

Ingredients

   1 small head of leaf lettuce, red-tip lettuce, or romaine

   1/2 of a 16-ounce bag of spinach
   1 carrot
   3-4 green onions
   6-8 cherry tomatoes
   About 1/2 cup of your favorite dressing, such as our homemade ranch dressing
   Ready-made croutons from the grocery store or unsalted sunflower seeds

Cooking Tools

   Salad spinner (if you have one) or dishtowels and paper towels
   Colander or strainer
   Large salad bowl
   Salad fork and spoon or two large spoons for tossing
   Vegetable peeler
   Sharp knife and cutting board

How to Make It

1. First, wash the greens. To do this, fill the sink or a dishpan full of cold water. Separate the leaves of the greens, throw away any tough stems or wilted leaves, and put them in the water. Swish them all around for a minute, then lift them out into a colander or strainer. (The inside bowl of the salad spinner will work.) Let the water out of the sink. If there is any sand or dirt in the bottom of the sink, clean it out and wash the greens again.

2. When the greens are clean, you need to dry the leaves so that dressing will stick to them. If you have a salad spinner in your house, use that—just pull the little handle and spin the greens dry. Or use a paper towel or clean dishcloth to dry the leaves. (They don't have to be completely dry, just not wet and dripping!) If you're not going to make a salad right away, wrap the leaves in a dishcloth or paper towel, put them in a plastic bag, and store them in the refrigerator.

3. Place the dressing in the bottom of a large salad bowl. Peel the carrot and cut off the stem end, then use the vegetable peeler to peel long strips of carrot into the dressing. Slice the green onions and put them in the dressing. Cut each cherry tomato in half and put the halves in the dressing. Use the salad fork and spoon or the two spoons to toss all the ingredients together. Let them sit in the dressing for about five minutes before finishing the salad.

4. Right before you're ready to serve the salad, tear the salad greens into bite-sized pieces and put them in the salad bowl. Now toss the salad again until every piece is coated with the dressing. (My Grammie always says, "Toss and toss until you think it's done—then toss some more!") Add the croutons or seeds, then toss just a little bit more.

Make-Your-Own Ranch Dressing or Dip

If ranch is your favorite dressing, it's easy to make your own! To make a ranch dip, just use sour cream instead of buttermilk. You'll make about 2 cups of dressing or dip.

Ingredients

1 cup mayonnaise or lowfat mayonnaise
1 cup buttermilk (for dressing) or lowfat sour cream (for dip)
2 tablespoons onion powder
1 tablespoon dried parsley flakes
1/4 teaspoon garlic powder
1/4 teaspoon salt
1/4 teaspoon black pepper

Cooking Tools

Small or medium-sized bowl and wire whisk or clean jar with a lid (like an old peanut-butter jar)

How to Make It

1. Put all the ingredients together in the bowl or jar. (The dip is easier to make in a bowl.) Stir or shake until all the ingredients are blended together. Chill in the refrigerator before serving.

Oven Fries

These are salty and a little spicy and oh, so good! They're Elizabeth's favorite kind of potato. Each potato should make enough to serve 1 person—unless the potatoes are really, really big!

Ingredients

Brown-skinned baking potatoes, as many as you want
Olive-oil nonstick spray
Regular or seasoned salt (try different kinds)
A little black pepper
Chili powder (if you like it) or paprika

Cooking Tools

Vegetable brush
Sharp knife
Cutting board
Cookie sheet or jelly-roll pan
Spatula

How to Make It

1. Preheat the oven to 375 degrees. Spray the cookie sheet with the nonstick spray.

2. Scrub the potatoes with a brush and dry them. Then put each potato on the cutting board and cut it in half lengthwise. Cut each half into four long wedges.

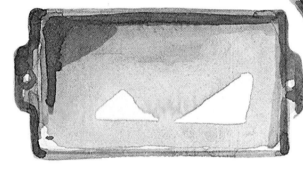

3. Put the potato wedges on the cookie sheet with the skin side down and the "points" up. Leave a little space between each one. Spray all of them with a little more nonstick spray. Then sprinkle them with salt, pepper, and either chili powder or paprika.

4. Put the cookie sheet in the oven and let the potatoes cook for about 30 minutes. Take the pan out of the oven and check the fries. If some are getting brown and others aren't, move them around a little in the pan. Then spray all of them with a little more cooking spray. Put them back in the oven for another 15-30 minutes, until they are golden brown and crispy. Take them out of the oven and use a spatula to put them on a plate.

Fun Ideas for Loving Your Veggies

• Did you know you can decorate with veggies? Just a few cutting tricks will make pretty vegetable shapes.

Cucumber wheels. Use a vegetable peeler to peel long stripes on the sides of a cucumber. Then slice the cucumber into wheels about 1/2 inch thick. The wheels will have a pretty striped edge.

Carrot curls. Use a vegetable peeler to peel a large, fat carrot. Then use the peeler to peel off big strips of carrot. Drop the strips into ice water and watch them curl up.

Celery brushes. Cut the celery into pieces about 4 inches long. Then make a lot of little cuts about 2 inches long down one end of the celery. Drop the pieces of celery into ice water and the cut end will fan out into little brushes.

Radish flowers. Cut any roots off the radish and hold it upright, with the root end down. Now carefully slice the top of the radish as shown in the picture—don't cut all the way through to the stem end. You can make "roses" and "chrysanthemums" this way. Drop the radish into the ice water to open up into flowers.

Tomato roses. With a paring knife, carefully remove the peel of a medium-sized tomato. Start at the top and cut around and around so the peel comes off in one piece. Then arrange the peel into a rose shape.

• Here's a really quick carrot recipe you'll like even if you don't like carrots. Peel a carrot and grate it using the biggest holes on the grater. Put the grated carrot in a microwave-safe dish, add just a sprinkle of water, and cover with plastic wrap. Cook on high for about 3-4 minutes, remove the plastic wrap carefully, and sprinkle the carrots with orange juice. That's all. The carrots are ready to eat.

• If you you're looking at a rainy Saturday with nothing to do, why not make fruit and veggie sculptures. Use toothpicks to hold various veggies together to make animals, people, or aliens. Cut little pieces to make eyes, noses, and hair. Be creative. When you're through, take a picture of your masterpiece, then pull it apart and eat it!

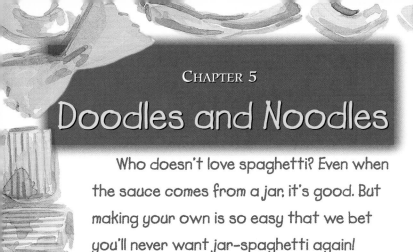

CHAPTER 5

Doodles and Noodles

Who doesn't love spaghetti? Even when the sauce comes from a jar, it's good. But making your own is so easy that we bet you'll never want jar-spaghetti again!

How to Make Perfect Pasta

8 ounces of dried pasta will usually make about 4 servings of cooked pasta.

Ingredients

Any kind of dried pasta—spaghetti, macaroni, or even flat noodles
Water to cook it in—3 quarts for every 8 ounces of pasta
A little vegetable oil, such as olive oil

Cooking Tools

Big pot
Long-handled spoon or pasta fork
Colander to drain the pasta

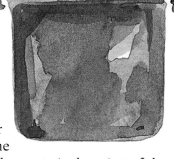

How to Make It

1. To cook the pasta, fill the pot with water and bring it to a boil. Add just a little olive oil to the water (maybe a teaspoon) to keep the pasta from sticking together.

2. When the water is boiling, add the pasta to the pot. If you are making spaghetti, and the spaghetti is too long for the pot, you can break it into smaller pieces. Or do what the Italians do. Hold a bunch of spaghetti by one end and put the other end into the water until it gets soft enough to bend. Watch out for the hot steam, though. This would be a good place to get adult help.

3. When all the pasta is in the water, give it a quick stir to separate the strands. Then let the pasta cook in the boiling water for a few minutes until it's done. How do you know? Check the package the pasta came in for cooking times. But the best way to know if the pasta is done is to fish out one piece carefully, rinse it in cold water to cool it, and then bite into it. If you are going to put sauce on it and eat it, it should be *al dente*—soft enough to eat but still a little chewy. If you're going to put it in a casserole or salad, you should stop cooking when it's just a little harder. If the pasta isn't done yet, let it cook two more minutes and then test it again. But don't let it cook too long—you don't want it to be mushy.

4. When the pasta is done, turn off the heat and put the colander in the sink. Have an adult pour the cooked pasta into the colander to

drain out the water. ☞ If you are not going to eat the pasta right away, run a little cold water over it to stop the cooking.

Not-from-a-Jar Spaghetti Sauce

Mama Mia! This spaghetti sauce is good. Aleesha's dad showed us how to make it. This recipe will serve 4-6 people.

Ingredients

1 pound lean ground beef or ground turkey
1/2 cup frozen cut-up onion, 2 tablespoons dried minced onion, or 1 tablespoon onion powder (if you like onion)
1 small green pepper, chopped (if you like green pepper)
1/8 teaspoon garlic powder, or 1/2 teaspoon chopped garlic from a jar
1 28-ounce can Italian-style plum tomatoes in their liquid
1 6-ounce can tomato paste
1 tablespoon dried parsley flakes
3/4 teaspoon Italian seasoning
1/2 teaspoon salt
1/4 teaspoon ground pepper
Nonstick cooking spray

Cooking Tools

Large frying pan
Large metal or wooden stirring spoon

How to Make It

1. Spray the frying pan with cooking spray and put it on the stove to heat on medium-high. Put the ground meat into the frying pan and break it into little pieces with the stirring spoon. Add the onion and green pepper if you like them. Then cook the ingredients together until the meat loses all its pink color, stirring every once in awhile. (Hold the handle of the skillet with one hand while you stir—and use a pot holder if the handle is made of metal.) ☞

2. When the meat is done, use your spoon to push it all over to one side, and tilt the pan just a little to the other side. Do you see a little puddle of grease? If so, take the pan off the heat, turn the stove off, then ask an adult to help you spoon out the extra grease into an empty can or carton. ☞ Let it cool and then throw it away—never throw it down the drain.

3. Open the cans of tomatoes and tomato paste and add all the rest of the ingredients to the meat mixture in the pan. Use the side of your spoon to

cut up the tomatoes from the can and then gently smash them. Put the pan back on the stove and turn the heat to medium-high again. Stir everything together until the mixture starts to bubble. Then reduce the heat as low as you can and let your sauce simmer for about 35-45 minutes, stirring every once in awhile. When the sauce looks thick and yummy, it's done.

Sesame Twist Breadsticks

These are a perfect "go with" for a pasta meal, and they're good with salad, too! This recipe makes 12 breadsticks.

Ingredients

1 8-ounce can refrigerator crescent
    dinner rolls
1 egg
1/2 cup sesame seeds
Nonstick cooking spray

Cooking Tools

Small bowl
Wire whisk
Sharp knife and cutting board
Waxed paper
Cookie sheet
Spatula

How to Make It

1. Preheat the oven to 400 degrees. Spray the cookie sheet with nonstick spray. Break the egg into a small bowl and beat it with a wire whisk.

2. Unroll the dough and separate it into four rectangles. (It will already be mostly cut apart.) Place 2 rectangles together end to end on a cutting board, so you have 1 long rectangle. Mash the edges of the dough together. Cut each long rectangle into six long, skinny strips.

3. Lay the six strips of dough side by side on a sheet of waxed paper. Brush each one with beaten egg, then sprinkle it with sesame seeds. Turn the strips over and repeat. Now carefully pick up each strip, twist it several times, and place it on the cookie sheet. Place the strips about 1 inch apart.

4. Do the same thing with the other two rectangles of dough. Then put the pan in the oven and bake the breadsticks for 8-10 minutes, or until they are shiny and golden brown. Let them cool just a little bit before using a spatula to remove them from the pan.

Fun Ideas for Noodling Around

- Pasta comes in all shapes and sizes, so don't feel you have to stick to just one. Try shells, wagon wheels, linguine—whatever you can find.

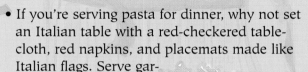

- If you're serving pasta for dinner, why not set an Italian table with a red-checkered tablecloth, red napkins, and placemats made like Italian flags. Serve garlic bread or crusty breadsticks, spaghetti with meat sauce, a big green salad, and spumoni ice cream for dessert. Play Italian music in the background.

- For a super lunch, try making a pasta salad. Just mix leftover pasta with some veggies (like peas, carrots, olives, and steamed broccoli), toss with your favorite dressing (like our homemade ranch dressing in chapter 4). You can also add goodies like sunflower seeds. Eat it right away or put in the fridge to chill out. Either way, it's good.

- If you add 1–1 1/2 tablespoons of chili powder and a can of drained kidney beans to your spaghetti sauce, you'll have a pot of chili con carne. It's good with pasta, too!

- Your sesame twist breadsticks can easily become garlic-parmesan breadsticks. Just brush with melted butter and sprinkle with a mixture of 1/2 cup grated Parmesan cheese and 1/2 teaspoon garlic powder.

When you suddenly go to someone's house and he says, "... You're just in time for a little smackerel of something." and you are, then it's what I call a Friendly Day.

Winne-the-Pooh
A.A. Milne

CHAPTER 6

Sweets and Treats

If you're looking for an afternoon snack or some goodies to serve your friends, here are some ideas we really like.

Fruit Dippers

It's fun to dip chunks of fruit into a creamy sweet sauce. We've given you three yummy dips to choose from—and you can use your favorite fruit to dip. This recipe makes as much as you want to make.

Ingredients

2-3 cups of your favorite fruit, including:
sliced banana
oranges, peeled and pulled into sections
cantaloupe or honeydew melon, cut in chunks
fresh or canned pineapple, cut in chunks
green or red seedless grapes, pulled into little bunches of two or three
apples or pears, cut in chunks
whole strawberries with their green hulls left on
maraschino cherries with stems left on
1/2 cup lemon, orange, or pineapple juice
Fruit dip of your choice

Cooking Tools

Paring knife to cut up fruit
Cutting board
Large bowl
Plate
Toothpicks

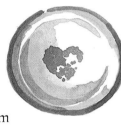

How to Make It

1. Put banana, apples, or pears in the large bowl and toss with the juice. This will help keep them from turning brown.

2. Arrange the fruit on a plate so that it looks pretty.

3. Use toothpicks or your fingers to pick up the food, dip it in your favorite fruit dip, and eat.

Three Easy Fruit Dips

Ingredients for Nut 'n' Honey Dip

1/3 cup peanut butter
1/3 cup honey
1/4 teaspoon cinnamon

Cooking Tools

Small bowl and spoon

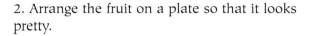

How to Make It

Just mix all the ingredients together in a bowl. This dip is great for apples, pears, and carrot sticks. Or try spreading it on bread and eating as a sandwich.

Ingredients for Sweet Cream Dip

1 8-ounce package or tub of low-fat cream cheese
1/3 cup undiluted apple juice or orange juice concentrate
Pinch of cinnamon
2-3 tablespoons chopped pecans (if you like them)

Cooking Tools

Medium bowl
Fork and spoon

How to Make It

Put cream cheese in a bowl and mash it with a fork until it's smooth. Stir in juice, nuts, and cinnamon and stir until combined. Try this one with pineapple chunks, strawberries, bananas, and grapes.

Ingredients for Easy Chocolate-Berry Dip

1 can prepared chocolate frosting
1/2 jar raspberry or strawberry jam

Cooking Tools

Large microwave-safe bowl or glass measuring cup
Rubber scraper
Wooden spoon

How to Make It

1. Spoon frosting and jam together into the bowl or cup.

2. Microwave on high about 3-4 minutes or until the jam is dissolved, stopping the microwave every minute to stir.

3. When the frosting and jam are completely mixed, put the bowl into the refrigerator and chill it. This dip is great with berries and cherries—or try dipping vanilla cookies or angel-food cake chunks.

Cinnamon Minis

These little baby cinnamon rolls are really cute. The best part about them is that you can make just a few for a snack or a whole bunch for a party. A recipe makes 60 Cinnamon Minis.

Ingredients

1 package refrigerated biscuit dough (the kind that comes in a round can in the dairy case)
1 stick butter, softened

3 tablespoons cinnamon
3 tablespoons sugar
A little flour for rolling the dough
1/2 cup powdered sugar for icing
Water

Cooking Tools

Rolling pin and clean surface for rolling out the
biscuits
Waxed paper
Sharp knife
2 table knives for spreading the butter and the
icing
Small spoon
Tablespoon for mixing and sprinkling
cinnamon-sugar mixture
1-2 round cake pans
Small bowl for mixing icing
Wire whisk for beating the icing

1. Preheat the oven to 400 degrees. Sprinkle a little flour on the surface where you're going to roll the biscuits and on the rolling pin. Tear off a sheet of waxed paper and put it on another counter.

2. Now open the can of refrigerated biscuit dough and take out one of the biscuits. Put it on the rolling surface and roll it flat with the rolling pin. Don't worry if it rolls around the pin; just peel it off. Pretty soon you'll have a flat, oval pancake.

3. When the biscuit is pretty flat, pick it up and stretch it with your fingers until it's a rectangle instead of an oval—sort of pull at the corners. You want a rectangle about the size of a 3 x 5 index card. Put it down on the waxed paper and spread it thickly with softened butter.

4. Mix the cinnamon and granulated sugar together in a bowl. With a spoon, carefully spoon some of this mixture onto the flattened-out biscuit. Try to sprinkle it evenly and thickly and cover the whole biscuit up to the edge.

5. Start at one of the short edges of the biscuit rectangle and carefully roll it up into a sausage shape. Lay it on the waxed paper with the "seam" down and gently stretch it with your fingers to make it a little longer and skinnier. Then use a sharp knife to cut the "sausage" into 6 pieces. Pick them up with your fingers and put them around the edge of an ungreased cakepan, sides touching. Don't worry if one of them "unwinds"; just roll it back up again.

6. If you just want a Cinnamon Mini snack, you can go ahead and bake these six now. If you're cooking for a crowd, repeat steps 2-5 until you've used up all the biscuits. You will fill the whole of one cake pan and maybe part of another. Let them touch, but don't crowd them.

7. Bake your pan of Cinnamon Minis for about 8 minutes, until they are puffed up and golden brown. Take them from the oven and put on a heatproof surface to cool while you make the icing.

8. To make Cinnamon Mini icing, put 1/2 cup powdered sugar in a small bowl. Add a few teaspoons of water and stir with a wire whisk. Add more water a little at a time, stirring after every addition, until you have a thick white frosting. (It doesn't take much water!) When the icing is mixed, use a knife to dot a little on every warm Cinnamon Mini. Let the icing set, then use a spatula to remove them from the pan to a serving tray—or to your mouth!

Fun Ideas for Easy Snacks

• Did you know you can make darling little cupcakes that look like ice cream cones? Just follow the directions on a box of cake mix to make a smooth batter and heat the oven to 350 degrees. Then, instead of pouring the batter into cake pans, pour it into flat-bottomed ice-cream cones. Fill each cone up to about 1 inch from the top. Put the filled cones on a cookie sheet or muffin pan and bake in the preheated oven for about 30 minutes. Let your cake-cones cool completely, then spread the tops with canned frosting. Decorate with chopped nuts, sprinkles, small candies—or even a cherry on top!

• Microwave nachos make yummy snacks. Just put a layer of tortilla chips on a plate, add a bit of shredded cheese to each one, and microwave on high until the cheese is melted. Top each nacho with a black olive slice, a piece of green chili or pickled red pepper, or be very, very brave and put on a pickled jalapeno slice. (Jasmine actually *likes* them.) You can make nachos with crackers, too.

• For a rich, fruity smoothie, just mix together 1 1/2 cups of lowfat vanilla yogurt with 1/2 cup of milk in a blender. Then turn the blender on high and carefully add about 2 cups of fresh, frozen, or canned fruit—such as strawberries, banana, pineapple, or peaches. (My favorite is frozen strawberries and bananas!) Cut the fruit into chunks if it's big and add it to the blender a few pieces at a time. Frozen fruit will take longer to blend in, but it makes a cool, rich smoothie! When the fruit is all blended in, add honey or sugar and blend until the smoothie is sweet enough for you. Be sure the blender stops completely before you reach in to taste!

• Do you like spicy party mixes made out of cereals and snack crackers? They're easy to make. Just mix together about 5 cups of different ingredients—like wheat or corn squares, oat "o"s, pretzels, or even chow-mein noodles. Then mix together 1/3 cup melted butter ?, 4 teaspoons Worcestershire or soy sauce, and about 3 teaspoons of flavored salt—like onion, garlic, and celery salt. Stir everything together and spread out in jelly-roll pans or roaster pans. Bake at 350 degrees for an hour, stirring every 10 minutes.

29

How-tos and Helpful Hints

Here are some basic cooking skills that will help you make the recipes in this book. If you still don't understand how to do something, ask an adult to help you.

Make Twice as Much Food (Double a recipe): What do you do if a recipe says it serves four people and you have five friends to eat with you? You can serve smaller servings. Or you can *double* the recipe. Usually that means you use twice as much of *every* ingredient—for instance, 2 cups of flour instead of 1 cup of flour. (You might have to use some math!) Usually you make the recipe just the same, but it might take a little longer to cook. Ask an adult to help you with this if you're not sure how to do it.

Measure Ingredients: To measure dry ingredients like flour or sugar, use plastic or metal nesting cups. Dip the cup or spoon into the ingredient until it is heaped up, then use a knife to scrape it off until it is level. Or put the cup on a plate, spoon the ingredient in until it's heaped up, then scrape off the extra.

To measure wet ingredients like water or milk, use a glass or plastic cup with markings on the side and a little extra space at the top. Pour the liquid into the cup until it matches the marking on the side. Read the measurement at eye level. That means you should bend down so that your eyes are right beside the marking on the cup. If you "read" the measurement from too high or low, it might not be right.

Helpful Measuring Hints: 1 tablespoon of something is the same as 3 teaspoons; 16 tablespoons equals 1 cup, and 4 cups equals 1 quart. For other measurements like this, look in the front or back of a regular cookbook.

Melt Butter: Measure the butter by cutting it off the stick (1/8 of the stick = 1 tablespoon) and cut into small pieces with a table knife. Put it in a microwave-safe bowl and microwave on low or defrost for about 2 minutes, until the butter is melted. Or put in a small pan on 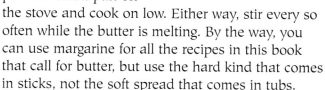 the stove and cook on low. Either way, stir every so often while the butter is melting. By the way, you can use margarine for all the recipes in this book that call for butter, but use the hard kind that comes in sticks, not the soft spread that comes in tubs.

How to Cut Up Almost Any Fruit or Veggie: Wash it carefully (scrub it with a brush if it's really dirty), and peel it with a vegetable peeler if you want to. Then lay the veggie on a cutting board. With a sharp knife, cut it in half lengthwise (the long way). Remove any hard seeds or dry membranes (like in a green pepper) and cut off any tough ends, bad spots, or roots. Then put the two halves on the board with their cut sides down and cut the vegetable into several more long pieces. If the veggie is fat, like a potato, turn the pieces sideways and cut them again the long way. This is a good place to stop if you're making veggies to eat with your hands. If the recipe calls for "chopped" pieces, first cut the long slices into really skinny pieces—about 1/4 inch wide, then hold several long pieces together and slice across them crosswise. The vegetable will fall into little pieces.

Helpful Cutting Hints: If you are cutting up bell peppers (red, green, or yellow), it's easier to cut off their top (stem end) and use your fingers to get out all the seeds. Then you can cut the pepper crosswise into pretty rings or lengthwise into strips. Green onions or scallions are tender, skinny little onions with their green leaves still on. You eat both the leaves and the white part. To slice, just pull off brown skin and wilted leaves, cut off the roots, and slice the whole onion crossways. If some of the white pieces are too big, cut them into smaller pieces.

How to Squeeze an Orange, Lemon, or Lime:

First, roll the fruit around on the table with your hands, pressing hard. This makes the fruit give more juice. To get even more, put the fruit in a bowl of hot water for five minutes, or poke it with a fork and microwave on high for 30 seconds. Then cut the fruit in half crossways (around the "equator"). If you have a juicer, push the cut side of the fruit down on the "cone" of the juicer and twist around to release the juice. If you don't have a juicer, just squeeze the fruit in your hands over a bowl. Repeat until no more juice comes out. If there are seeds, put the juice through a strainer to catch them.

How to Peel and Section an Orange:

Use a citrus peeler or the point of a knife to cut through the outer peel all around the orange, cutting from the "north pole" to the "south pole." Make these cuts all around the orange. Then use your fingers to peel back the sections of peel you've marked off. Peel off any of the white pulp that still sticks to the orange, then pull the orange into sections with your fingers. If the orange has seeds, cut each section in half and use the tip of the knife to remove the seeds.

How to Grate Cheese, Veggies, or Fruit:

The easiest kind of grater to use is the four-sided kind that stands up. Put it on top of a plate or paper towel. Pick the side of the grater with the biggest holes, and rub the cheese or vegetable against the holes to make shreds. Watch your fingers and don't grate them! When they start getting too close to the grater, get another piece of cheese or veggie.

How to Crack an Egg:

Always crack eggs into a separate bowl before adding them to the recipe. That way, if something is wrong with the egg, you can just throw it away without ruining the whole recipe. To break the egg, tap its middle against the side of a bowl until you see a crack. Then hold the egg over the bowl, put your fingers on either side of the crack, pull the shell apart, and let the egg fall into the bowl. This might take a little practice, but you'll get it right really quickly.

How to Drain a Can of Tuna, Veggies, or Fruit:

Use a can opener to cut around the lid, but leave the lid on. Use the lid of the can to hold in the contents of the can while you pour the juice into a bowl. Then press down on one side of the lid. The other side should pop up for you to catch hold of. Throw the lid away. (Careful! The edges are sharp.) Give the tuna juice to your cat if you have one. Save fruit or veggie juice to use in recipes.

A Mealtime Blessing

Thank You for each happy day,

For fun, for friends,

For food and play;

Thank You for Your loving care,

Here at home and everywhere.

AUTHOR UNKNOWN